COLLIN HOOLEY

CHANGES THAT HEAL

The Ultimate Guide on How You Can Effectively Change and Transform Your Life, Discover How You Can Change and Improve on All Aspects of Your Life to Become a Better You

Descrierea CIP a Bibliotecii Naţionale a României
COLLIN HOOLEY
   CHANGES THAT HEAL. The Ultimate Guide on How You Can Effectively Change and Transform Your Life, Discover How You Can Change and Improve on All Aspects of Your Life to Become a Better You / Collin Hooley. – Bucharest: Editura My Ebook, 2020
   ISBN

COLLIN HOOLEY

CHANGES THAT HEAL

The Ultimate Guide on How You Can Effectively Change and Transform Your Life, Discover How You Can Change and Improve on All Aspects of Your Life to Become a Better You

My Ebook Publishing House
Bucharest, 2020

TABLE OF CONTENTS

HOW TO GET AND STAY MOTIVATED

There are plenty of articles, books and blog posts on motivation that tell you how to become more motivated. Often, they give tips like 'getting more sleep' and 'introducing new habits slowly'.

These ideas are all useful to an extent but they ultimately fall short. If you struggle with motivation and can't keep yourself focused on new tasks, then a tip like this isn't going to transform your ability to focus overnight.

And if you struggle to motivate yourself, how are you expected to keep up the changes that lead to greater motivation? It's something of a vicious circle don't you think?

If you really want to see changes, then you need to look a little deeper. You need to focus on the actual neuroscience that underpins our ability to get and stay motivated. In this report, you'll learn exactly how motivation actually works on a biologically level and more importantly, you'll discover how you can manipulate that process to your own ends…

Introducing the Salience Network

What we're interested in here is what neuroscientists and psychologists refer to as 'attentional control' or 'executive attention'. This describes the ability we have to direct our attention and hold it – the control we have over what we choose to focus on and what we choose to ignore.

So how does this work? It comes down to several frontal regions within the brain that control this function. Perhaps most notable is the anterior cingulate cortex which has been the result of a fair amount of research.

In fact though, attention is controlled by two separate networks of brain regions in the brain: areas that work together in order to get the desired result. Specifically, these networks are referred to as the 'dorsal attention network' which includes brain regions that run along the top of the brain (dorsal means 'top' in biology – hence 'dorsal fin') and the 'ventral attention network' (which runs along the bottom).

Understanding these two different attention networks is key because they have different purposes that clue us in on how to get superior attention. The dorsal attention network is concerned with our intentional attention (bit of a tongue twister). In other words, when you decide that you want to focus on a book for a while, or you choose to check the time, you are using the dorsal network.

The ventral attention network meanwhile is used when our attention is directed beyond our control in a reflexive manner. In other words, when you hear a loud bang and you turn to look at it, that is your ventral attention network.

But your ventral attention network can also be distracted by a range of other biological clues. If you are hungry for instance, then your ventral attention network will begin to direct your attention toward getting food and if you are tired, then your ventral attention network will direct your attention that way.

So, if you're trying to get work done and things keep stealing your attention away, then it is going to be hard for you to maintain your attention!

The next question we need to ask is how the brain knows what to pay attention to. The answer comes down to yet another neural network called the 'salience network'. This network tells us what is important and what isn't and it appears to be very closely connected to our ability to motivate ourselves.

In other words, those with the ability to tell their brain what is really important will be able to stay focussed on work, they'll be able to run longer distances and they're be able to stay intensely focussed during competition.

But if you weren't born with a powerful salience network, then what can you do to fix the situation?

Taking Back Control

How does the salience network work? What does it deem as important?

The answer comes down to our evolutionary history. Every aspect of our psychology evolved the way it did in order to help us survive. Traits that proved conducive to our long-term survival would be passed on to our offspring and those that did not, would eventually die out.

Thus, the job of this network is to alert us to things that are important for our survival – which is based on biological signals from the body and our associations. If you see a lion, then your salience network will identify this as important, it will trigger the ventral attention network and this will direct your attention there.

The result will be that your parasympathetic nervous system kicks in and triggers a hormonal and neurochemical response: you'll produce adrenaline, dopamine, cortisol and norepinephrine and these chemicals will raise the heartrate contract your muscles and narrow your attention to that one thing.

To a lesser extent, this happens if you're hungry, too hot, too cold, or if you are stressed about something else whether that be debt, your relationship or anything else.

The first thing you need to do then to improve your ability to focus and stay motivated, is to ensure that you remove these distractions that can override your dorsal attention network. This means you need to create a working environment that will be free from distractions and that makes you as comfortable as possible.

Any loud noise, any discomfort, any hunger or any lingering stress can potentially make it hard for you to maintain your focus.

One trick that you can use in order to encourage a more focussed state of mind to this end, comes from WordPress creator Matt Mullenweg. He described to Tim Ferriss during a podcast interview, how he would listen to music he knew well on repeat. The music would play over and over again and he would become immensely familiar with it. As a result, the brain would then start to phase that music out. In other words, it would become desensitized to it, just as you eventually stop hearing the ticking of the clock. Only if you are listening to that music through headphones, it will drown out all other sound.

This effectively creates a kind of sensory deprivation. The only sound there is, is completely blocked out by the brain. You can achieve something similar by using white noise and this is something that many people will use in order to focus while working. Similar to white noise are other innocuous sounds, such as the rain or background chatter. Rainymood.com and coffitivity.com are both sites that provide these kinds of looping sounds for you to block out your surroundings. Similarly, using a widescreen monitor can help you to stay more focussed on work. Studies show that widescreen monitors can increase productivity by up to 30%!

But the most important thing you can do is to try and remove all other stress from your mind. That means that you need to try and stop worrying about your debt and even about the other work you have to do that day. If you are worrying about those things, then your brain will keep being distracted away from what you need to do. So, try to learn to block out feelings of stress and anxiety and to just focus on the task that is in hand. This may take practice, but this works much like a muscle – the more you train your mind, the greater the control you will get over it.

Jedi Mind Tricks

But we need to go further than this if we're going take complete control over our motivation. Ideally, we need to ensure that our ventral and dorsal attention networks are aligned. How do we do this?

The answer lies with the reason that we are distracted in the first place. The reality is not just that we think other things are more important, but also that we feel that what we should be doing isn't important. You might know consciously that you need to clean the house, go to the gym or tidy up. That's your dorsal network doing its work.

But your body doesn't know that. To your body, this is an unstimulating activity that isn't serving any of your prime directives. One thing our brain needs is stimulation and that corresponds with neural activity that comes from doing something that seems biologically important. This is why we find it easy to focus on computer games or films – they simulate exciting, important events happening, all charged with emotion.

Entering information into a spreadsheet though? Not so much.

But our human intelligence comes from our ability to focus not just on what is biologically important right now but on what we need to be doing in the distant future. In other words, it's our ability to extrapolate, plan and predict that has made us so highly effective.

This comes from our working memory, which is our ability to store information in our 'mind's eye' as it were. We can focus on things that have happened or that we think are going to happen and this causes the brain to light up as though they are happening. This is what our visualization really is – we're internalizing our experience so as to be able to manipulate the variables.

One way to give yourself more motivation then, is to learn to link the boring event or the thing you don't want to do, to the worthwhile and important goal that you hope to achieve.

In other words, you need to remind your brain why you are doing this using visualization. If you're sat typing out a spreadsheet, then visualize how this is going to eventually lead to you being wealthier, more successful in your career and less stressed tonight. Consider what will happen if you don't do it – you will be behind with work and you won't be able to accomplish the goals you're aiming for!

16

If you're struggling to motivate yourself to go to the gym, then imagine what it will be like to have rippling abs and a 10% body fat. Seem worth it now?

Another tip is to make whatever you're doing more interesting and more fun if you can, which makes it more salient to your brain. I always say that the best cure for writer's block in particular is to make the scene or the paragraph you're writing more interesting. If it's not interesting enough to write, then it likely won't be interesting to read!

If you're doing data entry, then make it a little more rewarding by putting some TV on in the background on silent – as long as it isn't too distracting to prevent you from paying attention to what you're doing. A good option is to watch people play computer games on YouTube, as this has no plot but still provides stimulation.

Oh, and once you get into the flow – make sure that there is nothing there to break that concentration. Put your phone on silent.

The Power of Meditation

Another trick is to practice meditation. Meditation is nothing mystical, it is all about focusing the mind and taking control of your attention. When you meditate, you practice clearing the mind of distracting thoughts and focusing on nothing. This is literally a way to train your salience network just as you might train your muscles in the gym and it can build great focus and discipline.

What's more, is that meditation teaches you to detach from those distracting stressors and to let go of things that might be playing on your mind.

Meditation can provide perhaps the biggest upgrade to your wellbeing, productivity and focus – so it is something that everyone should be doing.

The only problem? Meditation is hard to take up if you have low motivation! My tip then is to start out with just small 5 minute sessions and to try tacking this onto a habit that is already a part of your routine. If you regularly work out, then try meditating after your gym sessions. Or how about tacking meditation on after each tooth-brushing session?

And if you struggle to know what you're doing while you're meditating, consider using an app like Headspace (www.headspace.com) to guide you through it.

END PROCRASTINATION

Procrastination is one of your biggest obstacles to achieving what you want to achieve. So many of us have things we want to accomplish that we never manage to fulfil. Too often, this is mainly down to a lack of concentrated, strategic effort.

So, we maybe blame time. We might claim that we would love to start our own business/improve our home/write a novel/get in shape/actually clean the kitchen… but we just don't have the time because we are so busy with work and with looking after our family.

This is simply untrue.

24 hours (16 of which are spent awake) might not sound like that much, but it should be *more* than enough to accomplish all you hope to.

After all, didn't you watch a whole boxset of your favorite TV show only last month?

Didn't you complete the latest *Call of Duty* game?

Didn't you spend over an hour watching TV or browsing Facebook *most evenings* last week?

If you were to have spent all that time in a way that was useful and productive, then of course you would have accomplished your goals. And probably *much much more*. Heck, you would probably speak five languages right now!

Part of the problem comes down to procrastination. But really this is a result of some much bigger issues: those being energy and discipline. In this guide, you're going to learn to solve *all* of those problems.

Why You Lack Discipline

Procrastinations comes from a lack of discipline. This is what happens when you sit down to get some work done and immediately your mind begins to wonder.

This in term comes down to a couple of factors. For starters, the work you need to do is likely somewhat boring and unrewarding. If the work you had to do involved playing a computer game or eating a delicious pie, you probably wouldn't procrastinate.

The other problem comes down to stress and anxiety. When we feel anxious and stressed, our mind wants to turn to the source of that stress and focus on that – it doesn't *allow* us to engage in the things we need to do. This is why we'll often find ourselves killing time by browsing the web: it's a little like burying your head in the sand and hoping the problem will go away.

Of course, the irony is that delaying will only make matters worse!

Ultimately, this is an example of you *not being in control of your own mind.* This is the 'monkey mind' at its worst and it's a great example of how we can feel out of control when it comes to where we want to direct our energy.

And that brings us to the other problem: energy.

Often, we are simply too tired to do the thing that we need to do.

Perhaps you've just had a long day in the office and now you need to tidy up or clean the hoes. You're too tired to do that and so you think you should give yourself five minutes to rest first.

Which quickly becomes ten minutes, or twenty. And then it's bed time.

Heck, sometimes we lack energy and will-power to such a degree that we can actually procrastinate before it's time for bed! We actually find ourselves watching rubbish TV or browsing Facebook when all we want to do is sleep – because we can't face the thought of having to get up and brush our teeth.

And energy is responsible for this in a bigger way too. You see, discipline actually *requires* energy. Whenever we make any choice, making the harder choice actually requires energy. This is why we also tend to become *less moral* as it gets later in the day.

Our will power is fatigued at this point and so we'll often take the easy route – other people bedamned!

Now you know all of this, the next question is how you can go about ending that procrastination and gaining unstoppable will- power.

Why Discipline is So important

Willpower and discipline are actually two sides of the same coin and this is an area of your life that you should look to cultivate if you want to become a more impressive, powerful and successful version of you.

Discipline ultimately comes down to control over your own emotions and actions. And that in turn means you need to learn to stop being a *slave* to the way you feel.

We don't want to work through the night because it doesn't feel nice. And so we do it slowly and our mind fights us every step of the way.

The disciplined individual however can simply tell themselves that it doesn't matter whether they like it: it has to be done and that is that. They choose one goal, one objective and they shut out *all* other distracting thoughts and impulses.

This is powerful stuff because it allows you to gain laser focus over what you are doing and to complete any task. At the same time though, it also creates congruence in everything you say and do. People will notice that you aren't easily upset by things people say, desperate to please them, or torn about what to do: you are decisive, disciplined and immune to life's concerns.

This is *so* important. So often we try to please everyone because we want to be liked and we end up making weak decisions that end up upsetting everyone. So often we let our emotions lead us in our conversations and disputes which causes us to react badly in conversation. And so often we curl up in a ball and don't do the things that need to be done, which only causes our life to become more difficult.

The disciplined person rises above this and they are in *complete* control over their actions and reactions. So how do you become that person?

How to Gain Unstoppable Discipline

How do you gain discipline?

The same way you gain anything else: through practice and training.

And what this also means is that you need to recognize the discipline that exists in every moment. Discipline is the conscious choice to focus on one thing and to shut out distractions.

Distraction *is* procrastination and procrastination is distraction.

So, when someone is talking to you in a conversation, it is your job to focus acutely on what they're saying.

When you are meant to be working in the office but you're interested in what is happening on the other side of the room, it is your job to *ignore* that urge to look up.

When you are trying to exercise but you feel tired, it's your job to ignore the feeling and to power on through anyway.

It starts with recognizing that your feelings don't matter. As long as you're not hurting yourself, it doesn't matter if you're a little hungry, a little bored, a little cold, a little tired. It doesn't matter if you feel you deserve a treat. Being an adult is all about resisting that urge and on focussing on the things that you need to focus on in order to accomplish your goals.

This is a kind of 'incidental' training that turns all of your interactions and experiences into chances to hone your focus and discipline. But you can also set up further training opportunities throughout your routine.

One example might be to take a cold shower. Standing in a cold shower takes a huge amount of willpower and discipline and this is something your body and mind will fight you on every step of the way. But if you can force yourself into that cold water anyway, you will be training and harnessing your willpower. And actually, cold showers are very good for us seeing as they help us to produce more testosterone, they increase blood circulation and they train our immune systems.

Another example is to make your bed. This is something very simple but it's a great habit to get into: if you can successfully motivate yourself to make your bed every morning, even when you're stressed, even when you're in a hurry, then this will be great training to get yourself to do *other* things that you need to.

And guys: here's a big one. One of the most important things that you can do to enhance your discipline is to *stop* masturbating.

This is the power of 'nofap' – a movement that encourages men to stop watching porn and only to gain satisfaction through sex.

The problem with porn is that it provides us with too much stimulation and too much reward too easily. We have an amazing chemical reward 'on tap' that we can easily access at any time and this essentially trains us to give in to baser urges. We have no *reason* to wait, no work to do and no discipline necessary.

The same goes for any other 'bad habit' that you often give into – even if that just means entertaining bad thoughts. It may sound extreme, but when you indulge yourself physically or mentally, you are reinforcing bad behaviors and weakening your resolve.

This is why practicing various forms of abstinence can actually be powerful tools for honing your discipline. I'm not suggesting you become a monk – I'm suggesting that if you really want to kill procrastination, you have to learn how to avoid all manner of temptation.

The Importance of Reward

I'm really not telling you to become a monk here. While it's important to be disciplined and to fight procrastination, it's *also* important to enjoy life. And no one is going to be 100% disciplined 100% of the time – no matter what they tell you. Being too repressed and too strict can end up leading to more serious issues down the line.

What I'm telling you to do instead, is to give yourself rewards at *set times* and only once you have worked for them.

Want to eat a big chocolate bar? Sure you can. But only once you've gone a whole day keeping your calorie total to X amount.

Want to kick back and enjoy a good book? That's fine. But first you need to complete X amount of work so that you've got that under your belt.

Can't stick to nofap? Fine: but limit it to once a week at a set time and make it quick!

Giving yourself rewards for good behavior is a great way to motivate yourself and to allow you to add a little fun to your life *without* having to completely give up on being disciplined and strict.

One simple example of this might be with your daily work. If you normally start your day's work by getting a cup of tea and then having a chat, it's time to turn that on its head. From now on, you get the cup of tea and the chat as a *reward* for doing other good work. You're only allow those things after you have completed X amount of work. This motivates you and it allows you to work less interrupted. The same goes for checking your phone – put it on silent and allow yourself to check it once an hour for five minutes.

Doing this helps to prevent procrastination because your will power doesn't have to be so strong as to *completely* avoid ever doing that thing. Instead, it just has to be strong enough to hold off for a while.

One More Thing…

And one last thing you can do to train yourself out of procrastination: meditate.

Meditation is essentially an exercise in discipline. This is the practice of trying to remove *all* distracting thoughts for just a short period of time and using this skill, you can start to become *far* less easily controlled by stress, by tiredness, by hunger or by other impulses. Meditation makes us far more disciplined as well as much less stressed and far better able to concentrate and focus for long periods of time.

Of course that requires discipline in itself. Start with small five minute sessions a few times a week and build up from there!

OVERCOMING FEAR

Want to become the most incredible, unstoppable version of yourself?

I'm not talking about the usual 'self-help' stuff. This goes beyond being a little better with the opposite sex, or being a little more productive.

Want to take on all new challenges, explore new frontiers, grow and transform yourself?

Then the answer is to overcome your fear. Your fear is what is holding you back. Your fear is what is making you less capable and less formidable. And your fear is what is taking away from your happiness and your fulfilment.

It's time we destroyed fear once and for all and unlocked our full potential.

The Samurai Code

If we want to learn how to really conquer fear, then we can turn to some examples from history. Some of the most fearless, formidable warriors of all were the samurai. So how did they achieve this complete lack of fear?

According to legend, there was a technique that the samurai would practice right before battle in order to eliminate their fear. To do this, they would vividly imagine every possible way that they could be killed. They would imagine being impaled, dismembered and decapitated.

Then they would focus on accepting these possibilities and coming to terms with them. They would become okay with a horrific and brutal death.

The samurai were actually a very morbid and fatalistic bunch. The bushido code explained that it was an honour to die in battle and that they should *constantly* keep their mind on death.

You'd think this would make them more fearful but paradoxically, it empowered them to be the completely ruthless, fearless warriors that they were. This makes sense: if you fear death, then you will fear life.

If the samurai have accepted the worst thing that could happen to them and if they have come to terms with it, then what reason have they to be afraid?

Now imagine fighting someone who has zero fear of death: who is willing to put themselves at risk, to launch 100% into a movement and not be concerned for the potential outcome. They would be *devastating*.

The good news is that we live in a much less dangerous time and you probably *don't* need to come to terms with your death in quite the same way. But we can take this same notion and we can look at ways to apply it to our own lives.

Learning from the Stoics

Interestingly, stoic philosophers took a similar worldview when it came to their fears. Stoics believed that the secret to happiness was to be prepared for all the worst possible outcomes and to live inside those possibilities. They thought that blind optimism was one of the quickest ways to leave yourself miserable and disappointed.

Think about it: if you constantly expect the worst and get the best, then you are going to find yourself feeling either pleasantly surprised *or* getting what you expect.

If you constantly expect the best and get the worst, you are going to be consistently disappointed.

If you accept that negative things happen and you've *prepared* for them, then there is no reason not to take chances and risks.

And there is a beauty in things going wrong. The saddest points of our lives are rich with emotion because we have lost things we cared about. The only way to avoid that is to lived a bland and unexciting life. The moments when we have felt sacred for our lives have been the times our biology and psychology were tested and we had to use our wits and our courage to survive.

The stoics pointed out that the times we are most likely to curse the heavens are the times that we are shocked. For instance, you don't swear when it starts to rain – this is a normal occurrence and something we anticipate. You swear when you burn your hand because you were surprised.

If you expect things to go wrong, they don't catch you out.

Fear Setting

Tim Ferriss is the author who wrote *The Four Hour Workweek*. This is a book about finding ways to make your job fit around your lifestyle, instead of having your lifestyle fit around your work. This means deciding what you want from life and then creating a career that will work within that context.

Tim explains that many of us will remain stuck in jobs we hate and living lives that we find unrewarding because we're scared ofwhat will happen if we take a chance.

If we go travelling, our partners might leave us. If we take up a new career, then we might fail and end up bankrupt and destitute. If we look for a new job, we might get turned down by everyone.

Fear keeps us frozen and prevents us from moving forward. We are naturally risk averse which means we'd rather cling on to what little we have rather than go forward to win the big prizes.

To get around this, Tim borrowed the concepts from stoic philosophers and formalized them into a process that anyone could use to get over their crippling fears.

The process goes as so:

1. First, identify the goal or thing you would like to change. Let's say you want to quit your job and start your own business.

2. Next, write down all of the things you are afraid of and all of the things that could go wrong. First, your partner might

think you are irresponsible and they might leave you. Second, your new business might fail and you'll be left with debt. Third, your house might get repossessed. Fourth, you might end up vagrant. Fifth, your friends might laugh at you. Sixth, it might all go to plan but you find you hate your new position even more. You get the idea.

3.   Now score each of those things on how *honestly likely* they are to happen. Would your partner really leave you? It's unlikely unless there are problems in your marriage to begin with, so we can give that a '2'. Would you end up destitute or would you probably find another job, even if it's a step down from what you were doing before? Give that one a '3'.

4.   Next: do these things really matter? Score them 1-10. If your friends judge you... who cares?

5.   Now, you're going to go through that list again and you're going to write down all the ways you could cope with the things that go wrong. These are your contingency plans and the things that you could do to cope. For instance, if you ended up broke you could get benefits, you could dip into your savings, you could ask your parents for help, you could take on a part time job. If your partner left you, you could fulfill that dream of travelling the world.

6. Then go through the list *another* time. This time, write down all the ways you can mitigate the risk so that it is less likely to happen. Worried about getting into debt? Then write a business model that doesn't involve a big upfront expense and bootstrap your way to success. Worried about leaving your job? Then start your business in your free time first.

Now you're going to do something else: you're going to think about the worst case scenario if you *don't* follow through with your plan.

That might be that you end up stuck in a job you hate. That one day you'll be 80 years old and you'll look back on your life and feel that you never made anything of it. That your body and your mind atrophied from lack of challenge or experience.

What's worse? I know how I feel!

And focus on what we discussed on that section on stoicism: bad things *will* happen. You can't possibly avoid all bad things happening.

Meanwhile, you are only responsible for your own emotions. You can't make everyone happy all of the time so don't even try. What you should focus on is accepting this reality and then just doing what you need to for your own emotional and psychological wellbeing in the meantime.

This is why Tim also has the mantra that you 'don't ask for permission, ask for forgiveness'. If your partner is going to be unhappy that you travel, that you take up a business… so be it. You can't live without taking chances because of someone else your whole life or you will be filled with resentment. And you could die tomorrow, or lose your legs in a car accident. Maybe your partner might run off with another man/woman!

How they react to your decision is up to them. But you can't let that define your actions.

You can't hold onto things just the way they are. You can't prevent bad things from happening. All you can do is live life to its fullest and richest right now. That's why you *have* to take those chances.

Taking Chances

The above technique can work when you need to make a big decision or plot the course of your life. But what about that acute fear? That short-term fear?

Here, the exact same process comes into effect. Scared to speak up in public? Then quickly run through that fear-setting technique where you consider the possible outcomes and why they don't *really* matter. You ultimately have two choices: stay quiet and *remain* fearful, or take chances and grow as a person so that you're less scared next time.

Thinking of doing a bungee jump? Then again, run through all the things that could go wrong and how likely/serious they are. Sure, the rope could snap or turn out to be too long, but you know that the likelihood of that happening is somewhere in the region of 0.0001% or less.

Not only that, but it would be over instantly, you'd never know anything of it.

And you can't live your life in fear. So, jump!

Returning to the stoics for a moment, there is a saying that you can't control what happens to you, but you can control your reaction to it. Keep this in mind and keep your *reaction* calm, even when the world is crashing down around you.

All of this can be helped with a little meditation, mindfulness and CBT. CBT is 'cognitive behavioral therapy', which is a form of psychotherapeutic intervention that recommends changing your thought patterns in order to change the way you feel and the way you behave. Techniques include the powerful 'thought challenging' which essentially amounts to fear setting. Here you simply look at the limiting thoughts and beliefs you have and then assess how realistic or valid they are. Sound familiar?

And unsurprisingly, CBT is one of the favored methods for overcoming phobias!

But something that is even *more* powerful from CBT is the notion of 'hypothesis testing'. This means that you don't just test the ideas in your mind: you actually get out there and test them in person.

If you have a crippling fear of public speaking, then you get out on stage and you *purposefully* give a rubbish speech. You experience that 'worst case scenario' first hand and you prove to yourself that it really isn't that bad.

In doing this, you can learn to desensitize yourself from the things you would normally find scary and you can become a much more fearless and confident version of yourself.

And this is really the very best way to overcome fear: it's to keep pushing yourself and challenging yourself. Keep subjecting yourself to the very things you find daunting. Fear is a good sign – it's a sign that you're growing – and the more you practice keeping your mind calm and steady in these situations, the more you will find that reaction comes naturally.

And one more thing: remember to breathe! Breathing deeply will activate your rest and digest system – the parasympathetic nervous system – and this will slow your heart rate and subdue your panic response.

Keep your eye on the prize: if you can eventually eliminate fear, you can take on *any* challenge and succeed.

SELF-CONFIDENCE BOOST

If you want to improve your life in every single way, then boosting your self-confidence is one of *the* best ways to do that. With low self-esteem you're going to find yourself feeling bad about yourself and everything you do will be less enjoyable.

At the same time though, low self-esteem is something that you will 'give off' to others. This radiates from you whether you mean for it to or not and in turn, this can weaken the impact you have on others. Looking to get a promotion? Low self-esteem will communicate that you aren't sure you can do what needs to be done to your employers and they will feel less confident about giving you that boost in responsibility.

Want to succeed in your love life? Low self-esteem sends a powerful signal that you are not a good catch. Clearly *you* do not think you are a good catch, so why would that other person think you are a good catch?

This can eventually lead to a self-fulfilling prophecy. If you act as though you are worthless and if you don't take chances, then people will treat you as though you're worthless and you won't find opportunities. You will thus get further and further behind your contemporaries and that will only *worsen* your self-esteem.

So how can you get out of this rut? What is the answer?

In this guide, we're going to take a look at what you can do to boost your self-confidence and how you can become that powerful alpha male, or that dominant wonder-woman that you have the potential to be.

Why Self-Confidence Will Change Your Life

First, let's take a look at why self-confidence is *so* important and how it can change everything.

You know when you were younger and you fancied the boy/girl at school? You told your Mum and she said: it's all about confidence.

You probably thought that this was a lie: that really it was all about looks or money. Saying it's 'all about confidence' and you should 'just be yourself' is car bumper-sticker advice. It's a nice platitude that is ultimately just a lie to make us feel better about ourselves. Right?

Wrong!

Self-confidence really *is* what it is all about. I know some guys who are unattractive in the conventional sense, not wealthy and not in good physical shape either. Yet they get *loads* of girls and the reason for that is simple: they are outgoing and fun.

This is why 'bad guys' will famously get all the girls. These are the guys that don't care what others think of them and that do whatever they want/. This comes across as confidence and it happens to be *very* attractive.

The same is true for women. A woman who is a 6 out of ten can beat an 8 out of ten if she knows how to flirt (which comes from confidence) and if she dresses to impress (which comes from confidence!).

There is a caveat: if you lack *social skills* then no amount of confidence will save you. That is something else you need to work on (and you'll learn here). Otherwise, it's all about confidence.

The same goes for your career and the same goes for the way you fit in with your friends.

We all know people who are supremely confident and we know that they are highly attractive and highly successful. We all want to *be like* those people.

And the reason for this is that confidence sends the signal that you are higher in the hierarchy than others. In the dating game, we want to date people who we believe are 'out of our league'. This makes us feel good about ourselves and from a biological perspective, it is the best way to ensure our DNA thrives.

If someone has confidence, this tells us that they *must be* an evolutionary catch. On an unconscious level we are drawn to them because we think it will boost our status. Meanwhile though, someone who thinks nothing of themselves will be ignored and will be taken advantage of.

It sounds harsh but unfortunately, this is just human nature.

How to Boost Your Confidence

So how do you go about getting that boost in confidence?

There are two different avenues to take and these are external and internal. External confidence is much easier to acquire but it's the *internal* confidence that will make the real difference to who you are and how you feel about yourself.

We'll start with the easier, shallower option and then move onto the more profound change we can make.

Shallow Confidence Boost

The first thing you can do to give yourself an immediate boost in confidence is to change what you can about yourself to align yourself more with what *you* think a successful individual should be. For example, most of us feel that people who are more attractive and smarter are more successful. One of the biggest reasons that we might feel bad about ourselves is that we don't like the way we look.

So, the easy step one is to fix that!

One of the best ways to change the way we feel about our looks is to make some kind large change. A makeover might sound like a cheesy way to give ourselves a confidence boost but it really does work.

The key here is to be bold and to change things about yourself that you would normally be shy to change. You want to make changes that people will actually notice so that when you walk into a room, heads turn. You want people to think of you in a different way than they did before and you want to *feel* like a new person.

So, for women, wearing a bright red lipstick, wearing taller heals, or wearing a lower-cut top can all help, especially if these are things that you wouldn't normally do.

For guys, this might mean wearing a suit jacket, it might mean getting a much shorter hair-cut, or it might wearing a tank top to show off your arms.

Most of us can think of some outfits that we dare not wear but that we know look good on confident, attractive people. Guess what?

You're attractive too and the only thing missing is the confidence. Wear that outfit and you'll *look* that confident and that will make you *feel* much more confident.

Of course, you should still be you. So, don't wear things you don't like or that make you feel like someone else.

But just try to get outside your comfort zone and perhaps surprise people's expectations. Likewise, take some time to *invest* in yourself when it comes to your clothes and your grooming. Spend a little more money on better quality fabrics, take the time to do your hair and to moisturize. If you show that you think you're 'worth it' then this sends powerful signals too.

And if all of this is beyond you, consider hiring a stylist! There are people out there who do this for a living and who can help you feel *amazing*. Women: consider going on a makeup course!

Now enjoy those heads turn when you walk into the office and *work* that look you have.

Intrinsic Confidence

This latter example of confidence building works because it creates a 'virtuous cycle'. In other works, one good thing is going to lead to another. You'll dress more confidently and that will make other people treat you differently. In turn this will make you *feel* more confident and you will start to *become* more confident.

But if you want to truly upgrade your confidence then you need to do more work on that internal feeling of contentment.

And you know where this comes from? It comes from learning to *stop worrying* what other people think.

This is what confidence really is. The most confident person in the room is the person who spreads themselves out in a way that isn't done to make them 'look more impressive' but which is done in a way that makes them *feel comfortable regardless of what others think*.

The truly impressive person is the person who isn't afraid of upsetting someone with what they say. They aren't about to agree with the general consensus just so that they can feel liked. They speak their mind – while of course still being respectful to others.

So how can you get to this stage? Where you genuinely stop caring what others think?

The answer is that you have to know yourself and you have to know what's important to you. Spend some time reflecting and finding what your life's 'goal' is, what your true purpose is and what you want to accomplish.

Once you've done this, you will be able to start working toward that goal and focussing your energy on those things that matter to you. And once you've done *that*, you will be able to shrug off the insults or the opinions of others.

People are teasing you for being short? What does it matter when your goal is to become a great writer?

Not sure if a group of people like you? What does it matter when you know who your true friends are?

Knowing yourself and judging yourself by your *own standards* will make you immune to the judgements of others and will help you to strengthen your resolve and your determination.

And now, you will become someone who is much more interesting and much more engaging. Your passion will be apparent in the way you speak and the fact that you *aren't* so worried about what other people think of you will make you much more enigmatic and interesting. People you aren't trying to please everyone around you, other people are going to start trying to please *you*.

And this is the route of supreme, bulletproof confidence.

Training Your Confidence

Like everything else, this confidence won't appear overnight. It needs to be trained and it needs to be practiced. And this works just like training for anything else: on the basis of the SAID principle.

SAID stands for 'Specific Adaptations to Imposed Demands'. In other words, we become better at doing whatever it is that we do often. If you want to be more confident and stop worrying about what others think, then you need to subject yourself to things that you would normally find daunting and continually reinforce your positive feelings.

If you are usually too shy and unconfident to speak in public for example, this is going to be the *perfect* way to practice your new esteem. Force yourself to speak up in front of people. Better yet, force yourself to *get it wrong* on purpose so that you learn to face the music. Remind yourself: it doesn't matter what these people think and the worst that can happen is that you bemuse a stranger.

Practice talking to people and striking up conversation and always remind yourself that it doesn't matter what happens. You are developing yourself into the person that you want to be and that is *all* that matters. You can even try joining classes – a stand-up comedy class or a drama class can be a great way to lose inhibitions for example.

Meditation and CBT (cognitive behavioral therapy) can also help you to learn to react appropriately to the comments and reactions of others and to focus more on what really matters *to you*.

If you can do that, you'll find that you eventually start to like yourself. You're meeting the standards you set for yourself and you are thriving as a result.

In order to dress in that bold and more colorful way, you need to stop worrying about what others might think and instead focus on how it makes you *feel*.

And once you get a *little* bit of confidence like this, you'll find that it begins to grow and grow into something huge. Everything you do will be reinforced by those around you and each win will only give you more confidence to focus on *more* challenges.

A HEALTHIER YOU

If you want to become a better version of yourself and begin a transformation that will reach into every aspect of your life, then one of the most important places to start is with your health.

Your health is the source of *all* your power. The way you feel when you wake up first thing in the morning is what will determine how much you can get done that day. Your health impacts directly on your mood, your ability to complete physically or mentally demanding tasks and even your looks. Then there's the fact that your health will determine how *long* you live and the quality of your life *during* that span.

In other words, your health is the single most important thing to consider if you want to make life objectively better. And yet it's something that many of us don't give any thought to.

Seriously: most of us will give *far* more focus to our careers, whether or not the house is tidy and what our friends think of us than we will to our physical strength, the condition of our heart or how much body fat we're carrying around.

And it should come as no surprise then that a *huge* proportion of us are *incredibly* unhealthy. Many of us will drive to work every day and then spend *all day* sitting in an office in a hunched position while feeling very stressed. We come home and eat a ready-made meal which is packed with salt and sugar and zero nutrients and then we crash out on the couch before having a fitful and all-too-brief night's sleep.

Then we wonder why we are overweight, unattractive, tired, depressed and prone to illness.

Hmm!

The big problem is that many of us don't know how to go about fixing this problem and becoming healthier. And moreover, many of us think that getting into a healthy place is going to involve a large amount of work and effort – too much for us to attempt.

Maybe you've had a go at a new training program or diet at some point and found that it didn't provide the results you were looking for? Or maybe you gave it a go and then just ran out of energy early on?

Let's see what we can do about that shall we?

How to Think About Food

We'll start with diet because that is ultimately the easier thing to change.

Our aim here is health first and foremost, seeing as this will make weight loss and fitness easier. So don't focus on starving yourself – that isn't 'healthy' even if it leads to weight loss.

The key shift in thinking is to realize that food is not just 'fuel'. A lot of us treat our diets like we might treat the gas that we put into our car. We start to feel hungry, we start to tire out and so we realize that we need to refill the tank. We thus seek out any kind of food we can – preferably something that we will find tasty – and then we eat until we're full.

But food is *not* just fuel. More important than acting is as fuel, is the fact that food is also a material and a resource. This is what the body is *made* from. Our bodies work by taking what's in our diets and then recycling that into the raw materials that build our bones, our muscles and our brains. This creates the important hormones and neurotransmitters that enable countless reactions and processes throughout our body. And it is what we use in order to fight disease and cancer.

If all you think about is 'filling yourself up', then your body will be missing out on crucial nutrients and *that* is when you start to feel slow and groggy. That is when you start to notice your skin flaking, your eyes looking bloodshot and your hair becoming brittle.

Did you know that 80% of the US population is deficient in magnesium for instance? That is a *huge* number and it's devastating when you think just what this mineral does: it helps to form bone and connective tissue by helping with the uptake of calcium, it prevents muscle pains and aches, it accelerates learning through brain plasticity, it enhances our sleep and it helps men produce more testosterone for greater virility and masculinity.

This is just *one* nutrient and it does *all* that. Imagine the effect of not getting enough.

And then there is vitamin D: which we can get from the sun or a few dietary sources. Again, many of us are deficient thanks to our desk-bound indoor lifestyles, which results in lower testosterone production again, poor sleep, low mood and susceptibility to disease and illness. Vitamin D acts like a 'master key' for many of your hormones and helps to regulate your hunger and your energy levels among many other things. Studies suggest that adding vitamin D to diets could save thousands of lives each year by preventing serious diseases!

Then there's vitamin B12. This is a vitamin that enhances the body's formation and use of red blood cells, enabling us to transport energy and nutrients to our brain and muscles. Many people are low in this – especially vegetarians – which can cause nerve damage, depression inflammation.

I could go on and on. Essential fatty acids, vitamins, amino acids, minerals… all of them serve countless crucial and important jobs throughout the body and most of us aren't getting enough. That's because we're just eating processed sugary foods – things like cake, sausage rolls and Coca-Cola: empty calories.

So, there are three things I want you to do:

a) Switch to fresh, natural foods. That means that you're going to try to eat things that you prepare yourself from fresh ingredients at least four times a week. This doesn't have to be complicated or expensive. It can be as easy as having some chicken with a side of broccoli and rice, or it could mean having a salad leads with avocado, tomatoes and tuna fish. This takes minutes to make and it's not more expensive than a ready meal.

b) Take a multi-vitamin. While it's true that it is *better* to get the nutrients we need from our diet, many of us will fail in this endeavor and so we're left with no option other than to get it from supplementation. There is nothing wrong with doing this as long as it absorbs and it certainly can't hurt to *boost* your levels of those crucial nutrients.

c) Seek out superfoods and dense sources of nutrients. For example, you should consume smoothies occasionally if possible. I recommend swapping out your morning coffee on the way to work for a fruit smoothie (or better yet, a vegetable smoothie which is lower in sugar). Likewise, I recommend boiling a bunch of eggs and then snacking on them throughout the week. These are high in the brain boosting 'choline', as well as being complete sources of essential amino acids. Avocados are great because they contain magnesium, healthy saturated fats and more.

Finally, if you want to supplement your diet further, here are some things you can add that will help you to feel and perform much better:

• **Lutein**: Previously lauded primarily for its benefits for the eyes, lutein is a nutrient that can increase energy levels, as well as enhancing the brain.

- **Magnesium threonate**: Taken before bed, this will enhance your sleep and strengthen your brain.

- **Omega 3 fatty acid**: This protects the cells from damage, reduces inflammation (to combat joint pain and brain fog) and speeds up the communication between cells to boost brain performance.

- **Cordyceps**: Cordyceps can fortify you again adrenal fatigue and chronic stress. This is one of the biggest issues with our health today and by supplementing against it, you can increase your energy levels and prevent illness associated with being run-down.

The point is that by making these changes, you should start to look and feel healthier. You'll have more energy, a better mood and your brain will work quicker. This will then make it easier for you to start focusing on other aspects of your health such as weight loss and fitness.

Fixing Your Fitness

The mistake that most people make when trying to improve their health and fitness is that they aim too high. Their objective is often to try and transform their bodies into these athletic specimens that they see on magazine covers when they are currently barely able to make it up the stairs.

This is particularly apparent when running. Lots of people give up on running because they find it *horrible*. And they find it horrible because they push themselves too hard – they run too fast and too far because they want to become top runners or they want to burn thousands of calories.

But the best approach to running is to first simply focus on becoming *better at running*. Better yet, you should learn to *like running*.

To do this, you should go for shorter runs to begin with and you should take them more slowly. Go for a light jog through a scenic area and come home as soon as you stop enjoying it. Do this regularly enough and you'll eventually start to enjoy and look forward to those runs. This is when they can start to transform your fitness and your lifestyle.

Running once or twice a week even just gently like this will help you to train your heart. The difference this can make to your happiness and health should never be underestimated. When you run, you will specifically be strengthening and enlarging the left ventricle. The end result is that your heart will be able to pump more blood around the body with fewer beats. In turn, this means that your crucial 'resting heart rate' metric will slow down. Your heart will beat less as you train, which in turn will result in your sympathetic tone being better. In other words, you will be *less stressed* all of the time and your heart will be far less prone to hypertension.

But running might not be for you. This might be beyond you. Another great type of exercise to start up then is resistance training AKA weight lifting.

Weightlifting can transform your life and this is something that *far* more people should consider.

Many women – and in fact many men as well – will turn away from the idea of weight lifting because they don't want to become overly bulky or muscular. The point that these people are missing, is that it is impossible to 'accidentally' become too bulky or muscular. Arnold Schwarzenegger did not get to his size by accident! Rather, in order to get to that kind of size, you need intensive training and work.

A more moderate training program will simply give you tone, power and greater control over your body. And guess what? Building muscle will help you to lose a lot of weight because simply *having* muscle will increase your metabolism to the point that you'll be burning more calories even as you sleep. Oh, and it also gives you the ideal proportions you want.

A great training program for beginners to try is PPL – Push Pull Legs. That means you train all pushing movements one day, all pulling movements another and then legs on the third day. Again, don't push yourself too hard too fast. Focus on enjoying the training and just using your body in new ways.

You are *not* an athlete and there's no rush here. There's no reason to push yourself beyond what you find enjoyable.

Finally, note that you also need to be more active the rest of the time. Two or three one hour sessions a week will not make up for a sedentary lifestyle. So start to incorporate walking into your routine – this is a fantastic way to burn an extra 2-300 calories a day and that amounts to 1,000 to 1,500 calories a every work week!

Likewise, consider taking up a class, be that martial arts, dance or something else active that will get you into shape.

HOW TO DEVELOP POWERFUL HABITS

We humans are creatures of habit. We have evolved over thousands of years to like routine, to like predictability and to become ingrained in a certain series of events.

Most of us therefore have a routine that we pretty much follow every single day. Maybe you start your day by waking up, making breakfast, having a shower, getting dressed and then watching the news for 10 minutes with a cup of coffee before running for the bus.

You probably have a similar routine in the evening, which might involve doing a 10 minute shop at your local grocers, making dinner, watching some TV, having a shower and then reading a book in bed. You probably go to bed at roughly the same time every day.

This is no coincidence. This comes down to the entire way we are hardwired. The way our brains work and the way our biology operates.

Repeating the same actions or thoughts over and over again essentially means that we are repeatedly using the same neuronal pathways and causing the same connections to light up and fire. As we do this, those connections become 'myelinated'.

That means that they are insulated by myelin sheaths, thereby becoming stronger and stronger. If you repeat one action followed by another often enough, then often they will become so ingrained as to become automatic and beyond our conscious control.

This was demonstrated perfectly by the psychologist Ivan Pavlov who managed to condition dogs to salivate at the sound of a bell.

This is also why severely brain damaged individuals who can't remember their own name might still be able to play incredible piano concertos. Some can do this despite even not knowing that they can play the piano! The simple fact is that the motor neurons are *hardwired* over years of practice. The groove has been greased over and over again to leave a final impression.

As for our biology, this is based entirely around rhythms and patterns. The sun rises at a certain time and this triggers the release of cortisol and nitric oxide. These neurotransmitters trigger a cascade of activity throughout the brain which makes us more awake and active. Then we eat and this slows us down slightly again and gets us ready for work.

After 4pm, our lunch settles in and we start to become slower and more sluggish thanks to a dose of melatonin and serotonin. By the time the sun starts to go down, we are producing more melatonin and the build up of adenosine in our brain is making it harder and harder to think.

If you get up at a different time, if the sun rises at a different time, or if you eat a bigger meal, then this can throw that whole routine out of whack and as a result you'll feel out of sorts. This is what causes jet lag and it's why one solution to jet lag involves altering your meal timings.

In short, the more we repeat the same behavior over and over, the harder it is for us to change that behavior.

If the behavior in question involves smoking, then this is bad news. But if the behavior involves going to the gym, then it's *great* news. I have been working out at least four days a week ever since I was 13 years old (I'm 30 this year). That means that I've been doing something consistently for 17 years. As you might expect, I now find it almost impossible to stop. I love working out, it's a part of who I am and it's no effort for me to go to the gym.

In other words, harnessing the power of habit can be a powerful tool in helping you to get whatever you want from life: whether that's a better body or a richer bank account.

The question is how you go about forming those habits...

How to Create New Habits

The 30 Day Rule

Often you will read that the best way to create a new habit is to repeat that action for thirty days. If you can do that, then eventually you will have ingrained the behavior deeply enough that you won't be able to stop.

Is this true? Thirty days would theoretically be long enough for you to rehearse an action long enough for it to become ingrained at least somewhat, but that 'magic number' is actually very much arbitrary. There is no reason that doing something for thirty days should be any better than doing something for 29 days or 31 days.

What this idea does have going for it is anecdotal evidence: according to research, this indeed seems to be accurate and if you can stick to a new behavior for that long, you'll at least be on the right track.

This makes it a little easier setting out too. If you know that you have to exercise first thing in the morning for thirty days only, then that can be easier to stomach than thinking you have to do it permanently.

Micro Habits

Struggling to floss your teeth every day, even just for those 30 days? Then in that case, you might want to try using something called 'micro habits'. The idea of a micro habit is essentially to hack the 30 day trial by finding a way to stick to your habit for that long much easier and then extrapolating the results.

To explain, a micro habit means breaking down your new intended habit into something that is extremely easy and simple to stick to. So, for example, your goal might now be to floss just *one* tooth and to floss a different tooth each night. This is a two second job so there should be no difficulty in sticking to it.

But as with a 'full sized' habit, you should find that this micro habit becomes deeply ingrained after a while and that eventually you find it easy to stick to. Now all you have to do is to extend that habit so that you're flossing all your teeth!

A more realistic version of this might be if you wanted to write a novel, in which case you could aim to write just *one line* per night. Likewise, if you wanted to get into shape, then you could aim to do just 20 press ups every day.

This works best if what you're doing is still useful in its own right. If you only ever did 20 press ups, then you would still notice some improvement for example. Likewise, one sentence per night would still *eventually* lead to an entire book!

Try to avoid a scenario where you might look at your micro habit and feel that it is 'pointless' so you can just ignore it.

The great thing about micro habits is that right from the start, you are going to find you sometimes end up doing more. For instance, if you have set the goal of doing 20 press ups, you'll often find that you end up doing a whole workout any way – the hardest part is just getting started!

What's most important though is that you have the *option* to default to the micro habit. The important thing is that you are keeping this as a part of your routine – not so much that the habit itself (for now!).

Context

Another tip for creating a new habit is to try attaching it to your old habits and your surroundings.

In other words, if you want to create a habit of flossing your teeth, then a good option is to attach this onto a habit you already stick to: such as brushing your teeth!

Likewise, if you want to get into the habit of ironing your shirts, pick a specific point in the day for it to come *after* – such as making your morning tea.

This works because it connects the new behavior to old ones inside your brain. You have a network of neurons that fires whenever you make your morning tea. Now, when that network of neurons fire, they should also cause the new network – the ironing shirts network – to light up. The two are connected.

This also works on a practical level: you need to find a convenient time for your new habit to take place and you need to find a convenient time and place in which to do it. And you need to know that said time and place is always going to be convenient. You need to *always* be able to workout at this time, in this place.

I wanted to take up meditation a while back for example as a regular part of my routine. I struggled at first because there always seemed to be more important things to be doing and I could never find the right opportunity. So, what I did was to attach my meditation session to my workout session. I already worked out 4-5 times a week, so all I did was to say that straight after a workout, I would meditate for just 5 (yes 5!) minutes. That's a micro habit that would never take up too much time and I'd always be in the right place to practice it (the gym).

Keeping your environment and your surroundings consistent is also important as all the things in your periphery can help to encourage your habit. This is why when trying to *break* a habit, the advice is always to change your surroundings immediately. If you're trying to give up alcohol for instance, or drugs, one of the first things you're told to do is to stop hanging out in the same places and with the same people. These have become associated with the habit – these are now 'triggers'.

But if it's a *good* habit, then triggers are a good thing!

The Power of Routine

One action is a habit but if you string these together, then you have a routine.

I touched recently on the practical aspect of stringing habits together and knowing where you will be and what time it will be when you do that thing. This is incredibly important for accomplishing goals and if you can build a routine for yourself that contains *multiple* good habits, then you'll find that you massively enhance your likelihood of success in all areas.

For example, if you are going to start a new training program then you must know precisely when you will workout and where you will work out. And you should 'hang' this new habit off of your existing routine and actions.

If you simply say you are going to train 'five days a week' then this is not good enough: you'll find yourself putting it off, forgetting or feeling too tired.

Instead then, find a slot in your routine where you can always make space. For me, the best time to train is after I've dropped my wife at the station in the car. I do this every morning and the gym is right next door. All I need to do is walk over in my gym kit and then get started before driving home!

The fact that I'm already travelling means that there is no extra time taken up by the journey. And I don't wash until I get home, so I'm not washing more (which also takes time) either.

Likewise, if you want to stick to a healthy diet, then you need to identify when you are going to make the food and how you are going to eat it. I did this by finding a local salad bar I could go to on my lunch break. I knew it would always be there, it would always be cheap and I could keep it consistent.

Creating a routine is a *powerful* way to accomplish your goals then.

BUT don't forget that the value in life comes from mixing things up and trying new things. Don't let yourself move backwards, or you will start to atrophy and stop growing. Habits help you get to where you're going, but don't forget to enjoy the view along the way.

HOW TO CREATE A MEANINGFUL LIFE

What makes life meaningful?

It's a trick question of course. Everyone will have a different answer and there is no one way to live your life. Any answer would be just as valid and it's up to you how you choose to make your way in the world.

But there are certainly some things that *don't* make life meaningful. And there are certainly some things you can do to help you find your *own* meaning. In this guide, we're going to look at how you can discover meaning in your life and why that is such a powerful and important thing.

Is Your Life Meaningful?

Perhaps a good place to start is by looking at the state of our lives right now. Where do you get the meaning from right now?

There's a good choice that you will give some of the following answers:

- Career

- Family

- Friends

- Partner

- Children

- Travel

Very few of us will answer that the thing that gives life meaning is 'food' or 'computer games'. Somehow, our relationships and our careers take on greater importance and the same is true of our travel.

This roughly adheres to Maslow's theory of the 'Hierarchy of Needs'. Maslow was a psychologist and according to his theories, our needs can be plotted in a kind of pyramid with the most important at the top and the most urgent down the bottom.

Our urgent, basal needs include our physiological needs such as food, oxygen and perhaps sex, while things become a little more abstract and inspiring as we move nearer the top.

His pyramid looks something like the following, from bottom to top:

- Physiological needs – food, oxygen, water, sex

- Safety – shelter, health, avoidance of predators/aggressors

- Love/belonging – community, friends, family, partner

- Esteem – self acceptance, self-worth, confidence

- Self actualization

So the first thing we might note as being surprising from this list, is that love and belonging are *not* near the top – in fact they are around the middle. It is as though Maslow is telling us that love is not what gives life meaning.

Poets and song-writers might disagree but this is in fact accurate. At the end of the day, you can't rely purely on other people for your sense of happiness, meaning and accomplishment.

For starters, this is a recipe for disaster in your relationships. If *all* your meaning comes from another person and you need them for your sense of self-worth, you might well become possessive, jealous, clingy or otherwise toxic in that relationship.

Likewise, this leaves you incredibly vulnerable. If your meaning comes from another person and they should leave, your whole world will come crashing down.

You get people who have amazing, perfect, happy families and yet they don't have a sense of purpose of direction. They're stuck in a rut and they're unhappy because they don't have a sense of purpose.

In fact, this is incredibly common and it's something that a lot of us have to deal with. This is pretty much where the mid-life-crisis comes from!

Higher on the ladder we have esteem. That is to say that in order to be happy and fulfilled, in order for life to have meaning, you need to discover how to live with yourself and how to like yourself. Otherwise, you will be unhappy in everything you do and you won't have the tools necessary to take your life to the next step.

But that's still not number one. So just what is self-actualization?

The Monomyth

We can get a clue as to what might be meant by self-actualization by looking to the monomyth. The monomyth is also sometimes referred to as the 'hero's journey' and essentially, this is a common story that is told time and time again throughout history and throughout culture. We have many stories that we tell through movies, through books and through comics... but all of them ultimately tell us the same thing. It is the same hero, experiencing the same journey.

What is this journey precisely? It begins with the hero in their 'ordinary world'. Here we see them interacting with their family and friends as usual and we explore their surroundings. Then there is a call to action. Often, this comes from the hero's own need to explore, to journey out. It can also be prompted by an inciting incident though (the princess is stolen) or the death of a parent.

The hero then begins the journey by venturing into unknown lands. This is known as 'crossing the threshold'. The hero will encounter new allies, new opponents and new dangers.

Eventually, they will reach the belly of the beast – the most dangerous part of the new land known as the 'inmost cave'.

Then comes the ordeal. The hero faces an ultimate challenge against an insurmountable foe and usually, they are defeated.

Then apotheosis. This is the most important part of the tale, where the hero goes through some form of transformation and becomes 'divine' in many cases. They may return from the dead, or they may ascend and become *a super saiyan*. Either way, the hero is no longer what they were and they are now bigger and stronger than before.

They take on the enemy and defeat them and they journey home with their love/the elixir/peace.

This tale is told over and over again. Sometimes the story is fairly literal, such as in films like *Lord of the Rings* or *Star Wars*. Other times, the story is much more metaphorical or psychological. In a rom com, the hero is dissatisfied usually with their lack of love, crossing the threshold often involves deciding to pursue a woman/making a friend/trying to be 'just casual' and the apotheosis is usually an *epiphany* at which point the hero recognizes what they've been doing wrong/that their love was right in front of them all along.

Either way though, the single most important part of this story and therefore of *all stories* is the apotheosis, the transformation, the resurrection. This is the character arc and this is what gives *meaning* to the whole journey.

The journey *was* merely training to develop the individual.

And why do we respond to this so well? Simple: because it is *our* story. Because we are all that hero. We all set off from the relative shelter of our parents' homes in order to start a new career or attend college. Through doing this, we learn and grow and adapt. This helps us to find the job we really want and to get married and to have children. End of story. The most important part was our growth and our challenge – and moving *forward* toward that goal.

This is a hangover from our evolution too. In the wild, we would have begun life as part of a community and then would have ventured out in order to try and find more resources, shelter, food and so that we could start our own tribe. Along the way we would face challenges (snakes!) but we would have become stronger and smarter as a result.

This story is about growth, adventure, challenge – and these are the things that keep us moving forward as individuals and as the human race. If we stay comfortable, we never succeed.

The Evolutionary Shadow

Now it's time for the scary part.

If it is so deeply ingrained into us that we must go after the things we want in life, keep taking on new challenges and move out of our comfort zone to become something new… then why is it that so many of us eventually end up in dead-end jobs and feeling rather unfulfilled as a result?

This may come down to something called the evolutionary shadow.

Remember how evolution works? It is all about survival. The person who survives passes on their traits – which presumably are positive traits seeing as they helped them survive. Thus, all our DNA is made up of previous 'winners' and our psychology is optimized to help us live and thrive.

Problem is though, evolution doesn't care about us past 30… maybe past 35.

Why? Because once you reach that age, you've already *had* your children most likely (or you're in a situation where you are ready to). You've passed on your surviving genes and you've fulfilled your role. Therefore, it doesn't matter what happens to you after.

And this is seen reflected in the way we live our lives. Once we find a stable career and raise our kids, all the journey, discovery, newness and adventure is gone from our lives. We get into a rut and we start to move backward instead of forward.

The movies reflect this too: it's why there are so few stories about married couples. So few stories about princes that have already *become* kings and now must deal with the day-to-day administration.

And this is why our lives can often feel like they lack meaning. It's because they lack direction.

Actualization *is* apotheosis. Actualization is *growth*. It is becoming the best that we can be.

The quote often used to describe actualization is: "What a man can be, he must be."

If you are not fulfilling your potential, or moving towards a better version of you... then you are moving backward.

The brain literally comes to life when it has a goal, when we learn new things and when we give it challenge. It becomes more youthful and plastic as it produces more dopamine, more norepinephrine and more BDNF (brain derived neurotrophic factor). Our memories improve, our attention improves and we become more energetic and positive.

As soon as you stop doing that though, you greatly increase your risk of starting to develop Alzheimer's and other forms of cognitive decline. Your body is always changing and your only choice is whether it moves forward or backward.

How to Give Your Life Meaning

So how do you take all of this theory and turning it into useful practice? What do you actually have to do to give life meaning?

The answer is first that you have to recognize that having a happy family and a good job is not enough. That is important for your happiness yes: but it does not provide growth and it does not provide challenge.

In order to give life meaning, you need to become the hero again. You need to go on that journey and take on new challenges.

This can mean that you set out to make something amazing of your career – by becoming a rock musician, a top lawyer, or a business owner.

Or it could mean that you pursue a meaningful hobby. Maybe you write a book, maybe you learn to program and build an app.

Maybe you take up philosophy and try to answer some of life's deepest questions.

And it can be *about* family or charity too. You might decide to give back to your community or you might choose to have another child.

Maybe your meaning comes from your faith and that's something you want to explore. Maybe you want to see the world and save to travel.

But whatever the case, it needs to be a journey and a challenge. It needs to force you to grow and it needs to give you an end destination – even if that destination seems impossible. You must be striving, learning, growing and you must have something that you are truly passionate about completing.

Because when your life has direction, it has meaning.

It can be tempting to indulge in those lower layers of Maslow's hierarchy: to pig out on great food and to keep yourself warm, cosy and lazy. But while that might satisfy your body, it won't satisfy your soul. You'll slowly start to rot and decay and life will lose its color and meaning.

You will feel most alive when you are tested, tired, challenged and beaten... but you choose to keep on going. You will feel most alive when you conquer mountains. Leave your comfortable armchair, head into that inmost cave and come out more powerful than every before.

MASTER YOUR BRAIN

If you were to buy a car, a computer, a games console or even a toy of some sort, then in all likelihood it would come with an instruction manual of some sort so that you could find your way around it and how you should use it.

This is important because it allows you to get the very most from it and it allows you to avoid making mistakes that could damage it.

But unfortunately, the most important and most complex things in the world come with no such instruction manual. Take children for example: any new parent will tell you just how dismayed they were when they realized that no one could tell them how to be an effective mother/father.

And then there's the big one: our own brains. These are the most complex supercomputers in the entire world and they are what create all of our subjective feelings, sensations and experiences. And yet our brains come with no instructions and no guidance: we are left simply to try and figure them out on our won.

So, the question becomes: how can you master your brain?

Fortunately, neuroscientists and psychologists are uncovering more of the brain's secrets every single day. While there is still a *huge* amount left to learn, we know more than we ever did and a lot of this information can be used practically to help us become happier, smarter and more effective versions of ourselves.

Read on and we'll see how you can master your brain for complete and total self-mastery.

How Your Brain Works

Neuroscience is a subject that can take decades to learn and even then it will be necessary to specialize in one area – like I said, it's a complex piece of machinery. There is much more than can possibly explained here then, but we can nevertheless give a brief overview to give you some important clues as to how the brain *essentially* works.

So, what do we know?

First of all, the brain is made up of neurons. These neurons are cells that have long tendrils called axons and dendrites.

These reach out so as to almost touch each other and that in turn means that they will be close enough for small signals to jump across the gap. This in turn creates a huge map made up of billions of neurons with incredibly intricate connections. This network is called the 'connectome' and everyone's is slightly different. These individual differences are what give us our different skills and abilities and our different personalities.

Every single experience that you have can be mapped to one or more of these neurons. Each neuron represents a sensation, a memory, an experience, a feeling or something else. Your vision is mapped to a huge array of neurons that represent what you're seeing and likewise, your memory is made up of lots of interlinked neurons that reflect your thoughts and ideas.

These neurons are groups roughly into different regions throughout the brain based on their function. In the occipital lobe for instance we have all the neurons responsible for our sight. In the motor cortex we have neurons that correspond with movements and sensations throughout our body. Our prefrontal cortex is where we handle things like planning and motivation.

Our brain stem handles breathing. And our hippocampus stores many of our memories. This is why damage to a specific area of the brain can result in a loss of specific function and this organization is so extreme that there have even been cases where

84

a head trauma has led to a patient losing their memory of vegetables and *nothing else*.

Interactions between neurons occurs through 'action potentials'. These are electrical impulses that occur once a neuron has received enough stimulation. That stimulation is normally the result of lots of nearby neurons firing enough to put it past a certain excitability threshold. When an action potential occurs, this can also result in the release of neurotransmitters. These are chemicals released from vesicles (sacs) that alter the way that neurons work – perhaps making them more or less likely to fire, or perhaps making the event seem more or less important/sad/happy/memorable.

Another factor that influences our individual differences is our balance of neurotransmitters and hormones. If you have lots of the feel-good neurotransmitter serotonin, then you will be often in a good mood and you'll be relaxed. If you have lots of cortisol and glutamate, then you will be a more wired and panicked kind of person.

Neurotransmitters and Outside Influences

What's important to recognize here, is that those neurotransmitters are not *just* a result of what is happening in the brain but can also be a result of biological signals from our bodies. For example, if you have low blood sugar, then your brain produces more of the stress hormone cortisol. This is an evolutionary response that is intended to make us seek out more food – but it is also the reason that we tend to feel anxious and angry when we haven't eaten for a while. This is where the experience of being 'hangry' comes from!

Conversely, serotonin can be released when we eat something and our blood sugar spikes. This is why we feel good when we've just eaten. That serotonin eventually converts to melatonin though, which is the sleep neurotransmitter, and which suppresses neural activity. This is why we will often feel tired and dopey after a big meal.

Countless other things also influence our balance of brain chemicals. Bright light for instance can actually *reduce* the production of melatonin and increase the production of cortisol and nitric oxide to wake us up. Remember: there were no artificial lights in the wild and so our brain could rely solely on this signal to know what time of day it was!

While there is much more to it than that, this very generally describes the form and function of the brain and how it gives rise to our individual experiences.

Brain Plasticity

Another aspect of the brain that is very important to familiarize yourself with is plasticity. Brain plasticity – also called neuroplasticity – is the brain's ability to adapt and grow.

For a long time, it was thought that the brain *only* formed new neurons and new connections during childhood and after that point, it was set in stone. However, we now know that this process continues until we die and is a crucial aspect of the way our brain functions. It does slow down slightly in adults but it is still what gives us the ability to learn, to change our minds and to acquire new skills.

Neural plasticity occurs through practice, repetition and events that we believe to be very important. The saying among neuroscientists goes: 'what fires together, wires together'. In other words, if you experience something, a neuron will light up. If you experience that thing at the same time as another thing, *two* neurons might light up (or more likely, two groups of thousands of neurons).

If you keep re-experiencing those two things together, a connection between them will begin to form. Subsequently, that connection will become stronger through a process called myelination during which point the dendrites and axons become insulated to better conduct the flow of electricity. Eventually, one neuron firing will *cause* the other neuron to fire. This is how you can then learn a complex series of movements when performing a dance, or how you can memories words in a new language.

How to Hack Your Brain and Take Control of Your Performance

This might sound like a lot to take on board, but hopefully you have the basic gist regarding a number of your brain's functions. Hopefully, you also might have found some of this pretty interesting. After all, it is *very* relevant to all of us!

So now the question is how you can actually *use* this information in a productive way?

Controlling Neurotransmitters

One way to hack your brain for greater productivity, happiness or whatever else, is by influencing the production of neurotransmitters. We've learned that these influence our mood and our ability to learn... so changing the balance of these chemicals could certainly be very useful.

This is why a lot of people are interested in the idea of 'nootropics'. Nootropics are smart drugs – supplements and medications that can influence the production of neurotransmitters so that we have more goal-oriented dopamine or less fear- inducing cortisol. Modafinil alters the production of orexin, which can completely change our sleep/wake cycle so we feel more awake more of the time. This is also what caffeine does, by removing the inhibitory neurotransmitter adenosine (or neutralizing it, to be more precise).

The problem with this strategy is that it fixes the brain into a specific, unnatural state and prevents you from being able to easily 'switch modes'. No one brain state is superior to all others – for example, creativity actually requires relaxation, not stimulation.

Worse, the brain can adapt to those changes by creating more or less 'receptor sites' (the points where the neurotransmitters work) to make us more or less sensitive to the neurotransmitters in question. This can eventually lead to addiction.

Some neurotransmitters work better by focussing more on neuroplasticity, or more on energy production, but for the most part this is *not* the solution.

What is a much more useful solution is to look at those factors that natural influence neurotransmitter release. If you want to hack any system, then the answer is to look at what the inputs are.

So, we know that bright light can increase energy and make us less sleepy, so why not consider investing in a daylight lamp which is designed to combat SAD (Seasonal Affective Disorder) by simulating the sun's rays? We know that cold likewise can increase focus, while heat can help us to feel more relaxed and happy. We know that the sun and that exercise can boost our mood through the production of serotonin.

We also know that our brain is subject to certain natural cycles – those relating to sleep and hunger for instance. By timing our productivity *around* those things, we can work more effectively and freer from distraction.

And if you find yourself feeling very stressed or depressed, then it might pay to consider some of the biological factors that may be causing that. Perhaps you're hungry? Or perhaps you're a little ill and the pro-inflammatory cytokines are causing brain fog? Once you know the problem is transient and biological, it can be much easier to let it pass.

Controlling Your Brain

More importantly though, it is critical that you learn to create the moods and the feelings that you need by changing the way you think and use your brain.

The thing that makes humans unique is our ability to visualize – to internalize events and to imagine future scenarios or possibilities. This is our working memory at play and it is what enables us to think of long-term goals and to invent new ideas. And if you believe in the theory of 'embodied cognition', then you might find that this is even what we use to understand plain English (look it up – it's fascinating!).

When we visualize or imagine, we do so by lighting up the same neurons in the brain as though the event were really happening. Neurologically, we find actually doing something and imaging doing something almost indistinguishable.

This means that you can use visualization in order to practice things and develop skills – you can trigger brain plasticity just as though you were really practicing the event! Not only that, but you can also use this as a way to trigger the correct neurotransmitters in order to put yourself in the correct state of mind.

Ultimately, this will lead to the ability to control your own emotions to trigger the best possible mental state for the task at hand. It requires training of your visualization skills and the awareness to then *use* those skills to ease your anxiety and to motivate yourself to focus and to become more alert as necessary. This is the neuroscience that underlies psychological approaches such as cognitive behavioral therapy and philosophies such as stoicism.

This is *also* why it is so important to avoid bad habits – even bad habits in our thoughts – as ruminating and indulging actually strengthens connections that make those habits harder and harder to break.

There's a lot more to making the most from your own brain, but I hope this basic primer has given you a better understanding a little more control.

GOAL SETTING MADE SIMPLE

In order to get what you want from life, you first need to know what that is. How can you fulfil your potential if you don't know who you are or what makes you happy?

This is why goal setting is such a crucial skill to cultivate and something that everyone should spend more time learning. If you don't know what your goals are, then life becomes a little like going on a journey with no destination. Even if you might enjoy the journey, you're still going to risk ending up somewhere you don't want to be and you certainly won't take the most efficient route to get there!

So, it's simple right? You just have to ask yourself what you really want from life and then go and get it. Right?

Unfortunately not. Unfortunately, goal setting is anything *but* easy and is very much a skill in itself. The problem is that not many people realize this and they never think to assess the quality of the goals themselves. They blame their motivation, their circumstances or even other people.

But rarely do they assess whether the gault might lie with the goal itself.

In this guide, you're going to learn what makes a great goal and you're going to discover how to formulate goals and targets that you can *actually* stand a good chance of completing. Once you've finished, you might well realize why life hasn't *yet* turned out quite the way you want it.

An Example of Bad Goal Setting

To understand how to write a good goal, it can help to first take a look at what makes a *bad* goal. Why is it that some goals just don't work out the way they should? What should we do differently to avoid this happening the next time?

Let's imagine for a moment that you want to get into shape. You're planning on losing weight and building muscle – which is a pretty popular goal that an awful lot of people are interested in accomplishing.

In this case, a typical goal might involve writing down the ideal bodyweight and/or measurements that you are trying to reach and then setting yourself a target – 3 months, 6 months or 1 year. And then you get to it!

But this is a goal that is destined to failure. Why? Because it is far too vague, far too distant and far too out of your control.

Let's fast forward two weeks, at which point you have hopefully been training hard for a while and changing your diet. Suddenly, life starts to get in the way. You find yourself bogged down with other things you have to do and you just don't have the time or energy to make it to the gym today. Or tomorrow. And Wednesday is looking tricky. So is Thursday.

But it's okay. Because you don't need to work out. Not working out on those days is not breaking your goal. You have plenty of time to reach your goal and it is up to you how you are going to go about making it happen. So, if you take time off today, you'll just put some more time in tomorrow. Or the next day. If this week is a write-off, then you can always make up for it *next week*.

And so it continues, week after week, until you get to the end of your allotted time span and you realize you've blown any chance of accomplishing that goal.

Or how about this alternative scenario? Imagine that you *did* put in the time and you worked very hard every day to get into shape. But the pounds just didn't come off. Maybe this is due to a slow metabolism, maybe it boils down to people offering to take you out for dinner too frequently.

Either way, you get to a certain point and you realize once again that you aren't going to make it. *Even though you tried your best.*

So, what do you do? You give up, disheartened, and you leave it a *long* time before you ever try again.

A Better Goal

So, let's imagine that same scenario but this time write the goal correctly. What would a good goal look like if you wanted to lose weight and build muscle?

For starters, you should remove the time element. Instead of aiming to accomplish something in X number of days, how about you instead aim to do something *every day*. Look at the goal that you want to accomplish and then break that down into much smaller steps. In order to lose weight, you need to eat 2,000 calories or less a day. And you need to work out three times a week.

If you can do that, then you will *eventually* notice changes – be they big or small.

So instead of focusing on the end goal, set yourself a short-term goal. This is something that is entirely within your control – meaning that you cannot 'fail' for reasons outside of your control. It is also completely resistant to being put off or delayed. You can't 'work out today' tomorrow! Likewise, a slow metabolism isn't going to prevent you from eating only 2,000 calories.

Jerry Seinfeld explains a technique that he uses in order to make sure he sticks to these kinds of goals and he calls it 'the chain'.

The idea is that he builds a chain as he completes his daily targets and this then creates an immense pressure *not to break* the chain.

You can do this with a calendar and a pen. So, every day that you successfully work out, you put a tick on the calendar for that day. This will then start to gradually build up a row of ticks and over time, you will come to feel proud of that row of ticks and not want to ruin it by missing one. You won't want to 'break the chain'.

Whether you use this additional strategy or not, the point is that you should write goals that are immediate and simple. Meanwhile, you can let the overarching objective 'take care of itself'.

Is Your Goal Too Ambitious?

There's nothing wrong with an ambitious goal. Many people say that 'dreaming big' can even make you *more likely* to accomplish your aim because it attracts attention, gravitates people toward you and helps get people on board. If you tell people you want to fly to space, you'll get a lot more positive attention than if you tell people you want to climb Mount Snowdown (a pretty small mountain in Wales).

This is why another piece of advice that often gets thrown about is to 'have visions, not goals'. Visions are abstract and they are grand. These are things you visualize and dream about, rather than things you write down and tick off. If you want to get into shape, then your goal can be to train three times a week, but your *vision* would be to become the best physical specimen you can – attractive to everyone and full of confidence and energy.

But while a vision can be as grand and extreme as you like, those smaller steps should still be small and they should be easy. At least at the very *start* these steps should be easy and this will then allow you to build towards your higher overarching objective. Think of this like a hierarchy. At the top, you have your grand vision for the future – something so exciting that it helps you to launch yourself out of bed in the morning.

Beneath that, you might have your 'realistic' version of what you can achieve with your current resources. Beneath that, you might have the steps you are taking every day to achieve it.

The mistake a lot of people make is to clump all these things together and not to consider the necessary progression from one stage to the next. This is the reason that someone who has never been to the gym before, might well write themselves a new training program that requires them to train for an hour a day, seven days a week and to do this on a diet of 1,000 calories.

They'll then do stretching on top of that and start a yoga class.

Is it any wonder that we don't tend to stick to these goals?

The problem really tends to boil down to impatience. People want to accomplish their goals *now*. They don't want to put in the time or the repetitive work that it actually takes in order to get to that point. And they don't want the uncertainty that after all that work, it may *not* pay off.

But you need to change that thinking. Everything worth having comes with work and diligence and this is *often* highly repetitive and boring. If you want to get into shape, you need to train regularly and it takes years to get to a point where your new physique is impressive and 'permanent'. If you want to start your own business, well then there is a ton you need to learn before you even get going.

(Procrastinating on a goal is just as bad by the way though – which is another reason it is so important you have a concrete action plan!)

Think of this like a computer game. Computer games begin with a few levels that are incredibly easy and this is necessary to prevent you as the player from rage quitting. Your goals should be the same – if your 'level one' is a massive boss battle, then you won't be successful.

Lots of people get this wrong when they are taking up running for the first time. Here, they aim to start running long distances right away and losing weight. It's grueling, painful and unrewarding and it leaves them gasping and achy for days after.

What they *should* do is to to first focus on *getting good* at running and on *learning to like* running.

So that means they should be running short distances, not running too fast, not running too far and generally not pushing themselves beyond a sensible point. This way, they can gradually start to *like* running and they can gradually find themselves running further and further without even trying.

And in fact, often it only takes small changes to get to the place you want to be. This is best exemplified by the Japanese notion of 'Kaizen'. Kaizen essentially means 'lots of small changes that build up to big results.

For instance, if you want to lose weight, then it might be easier to look at small changes you can make to get there, rather than massive ones:

- Walk from the bus stop before your destination on your commute

- Stop drinking calorific coffees in the morning

- Swap sugary soda drinks for still water as your main source of hydration

- Take your lunch snack out of your lunchbox

- Eat off of smaller plates

These are just a few small changes that should be easy enough for most people to stick to and yet they can be enough to really sway your calorie total in your favor – eventually leading to cumulative weight loss!

Closing Comments

As you can see then, learning to structure your goals correctly can make a big difference when it comes to your likelihood of accomplishing them. The key is to set your sights high, but to have concrete, small steps that you can take along the way in order to get there. Forget how long it is going to take, deal with it being 'boring' and just focus on repeating the same few actions every day until you eventually achieve the thing you want to achieve or become the person you want to become.

And if you assess the situation in a year and you still haven't made the progress you'd hoped? Then perhaps you need to rethink those goals again. Like anything else, this takes time, practice and effort. But you're not in any rush!

CLEAR THE MIND

Your entire experience and quality of life hinges on your ability to clear and control the mind.

Many of us believe that our happiness is dependent on outside factors and on what happens to us. This however is not true.

Rather, our happiness depends on the way we *react* to what happens to us. And the same goes for every other aspect of our experience too: your stress levels are a result of the way you react to events, and your ability to be productive depend on your reactions too.

Don't believe me? To prove it, let's imagine that you're in a caravan and it's hanging over the edge of a cliff. If you move too much then it's going to topple over the edge into a ravine.

If you are aware of this situation, then in all likelihood you will be riddled with fear. Your heartrate will increase, your blood vessels will dilate, your muscles will contract and you will start breathing quickly. You'll sweat and your mind will be all over the place.

But now let's imagine that you're in the very *same* situation but you *believe* that you can fly. In that case, you'll probably sit happily reading and not worry all too much about your precarious position!

As you can see here, your belief about the situation and about the events is what is in control of not just your mood – but your very physiology. And guess which person is more likely to survive this situation without letting the caravan fall?

Now don't get this twisted: I am not here to tell you that holding completely deluded beliefs is the way forward! And nor should you convince yourself you can fly.

But this is merely a demonstration of the power of the mind and of your beliefs. Now if you imagine yourself in another more realistic setting you can see how your beliefs can change the way you react.

Let's say you're standing up on stage and you're about to give a speech in front of lots of people.

Some of us don't believe we can fly. Some of us think that we're going to say the wrong thing, that we're going to stutter and that people are going to laugh at us! We thus begin to panic and guess what? Our blood vessels dilate, our muscles contract and our heartrate goes up. Our mind begins to race which makes us *more likely* to make mistakes and our throat becomes dry and hoarse. The irony is that the speech is much more likely to go wrong simply because we're worried that it might!

And now imagine the same scenario but where you believe it's going to go well, or where you just aren't bothered about what other people might think. This kind of calm mindfulness is going to help you to act as though there isn't even an audience there!

Again, it is your reaction to the event that is going to keep stress at bay.

And it's not just these acutely stressful situations that can benefit from mindfulness and calmness either. Imagine for example that you come home from work and you can't stop thinking about the last thing your boss/client/colleague said to you. Then you wonder if you sent that important last email…

How present are you going to be when you get home? How much are your family likely to enjoy spending time with you?

Imagine that you are on a great holiday but all you can think about is whether or not you left the oven on at home. How much do you think you'll enjoy the incredible views of mountains going past your window?

Imagine that you're in the gym and your mind is thinking about the computer game you were playing last night, or X Factor. Do you really think that you're going to be capable of exerting maximum force in that workout?

Introducing CBT

Our aim is to help you to take back control over your mind and in doing this, you're also going to be taking back control over your emotions and your feelings.

The end result is that you're going to be able to become completely present in any given moment and completely 'mindful', thereby abandoning unhelpful concerns, stressors and emotions.

There's a school of psychology that can help us to do this called CBT. CBT stands for 'Cognitive Behavioral Therapy' and it's all about taking control of your thoughts. What's more, is CBT actually starts out using a form of mindfulness meditation.

Mindfulness meditation means that you are meditating in such a way as to become more aware of your own thoughts and feelings. In other forms of meditation – such as transcendental meditation ask the user to try and completely clear their mind, often by focussing on a single point in space, or perhaps a sound or a word (this is called a 'mantra' and it is why we imagine Buddhist monks to hum as they meditate!). The difference with mindfulness is that you aren't trying to eradicate your thoughts but rather you are trying to simply 'watch them' as they float past you. The idea is that you are becoming aware of the kinds of things you normally think but you aren't engaging with them and you aren't letting them affect you. The description is often that you should watch them pass by 'like clouds in the sky'.

Do this for a while and then write down the content of some of those thoughts. Look at the things you stress about and worry about on a regular basis and reflect on them in an objective, disconnected manner – nonjudgmentally.

Cognitive Restructuring

The CBT professional would next instruct you to begin breaking down and analysing those thoughts. Some of these will be things that you are going to worrying about and stressing about and which are going to stop you from enjoying yourself in the moment.

You're going to practice dismissing them but to help, you're also going to disassemble them using restructuring techniques.

One example of this is called 'thought challenging' which is going to teach you to challenge the validity of your worries or your distractions.

For example, let's say that you're worried you didn't send an email at work. Thought challenging is going to help you overcome this. First, you ask yourself if there's anything you can do about it. If not, then what is the good in worrying? In fact, it is more important that you relax and enjoy yourself so that you can be fresh and well to handle the challenges tomorrow.

Next, you ask how much it really matters. What is the worst case scenario? Everyone makes mistakes and in all likelihood, your boss isn't going to be furious – they'll be understanding.

Does some small part of you think that you're going to get fired? Then just remind yourself that this is incredibly hard for any business to do legally and it would be worse for them than it would be for you.

And after all, if your workplace would fire you so readily, would you really want to be there anyway?

Are you worried that people will be mad at you? You made a mistake! So what? And since when do you need to be best friends with your work colleagues?

This *is* the logical and reasonable reaction to this concern and once you can learn to deconstruct your worries this way, it will allow you to simply forget them and go back to enjoying whatever you're doing – or remaining calm when you're under pressure.

How to Use the Body Scan Meditation

Generally meditating is one of the most important ways to promote mindfulness, calm and self-control.

In his book *Tools of Titans*, Tim Ferriss looks at the habits and routines of the world's most successful people. What he finds is that they have a lot of things in common and one of the *most prevalent* of these commonalities is that they all meditate!

Everyone from Arnold Schwarzenegger, to Tony Robbins, to Elon Musk describe meditation as being a key tool that helped them achieve everything they did.

When you meditate, you learn a method to forget your worries and to simply let your mind 'be'. More importantly though, you develop greater concentration and greater focus which prevents your mind from getting into an anxious mess to begin with!

So how do you begin meditation?

One useful strategy is to start with the body scan technique. To get started, sit somewhere comfortable with your legs crossed and your hands on your knees. Keep your back straight, your chin up and forward and your eyes closed – but make sure you aren't in a position where you can fall asleep!

Now you're going to simply 'scan' your body by focussing on each part one at a time and then making a note of how it feels and relaxing it. Before that though, you begin with your senses. Listen carefully to the world around you. You'll find that there are sounds that you have completely blocked out until now and you'll notice birds tweeting, cars honking, children playing and wind howling.

Feel the temperature of your skin, notice if you're on a slight gradient and even look at the light as it dances through your eyelids.

Okay, now focus on the top of your head and start to take your attention downward to your cheeks, jaw and then neck and shoulders. Stop at each point and make a note of how it feels: are you carrying any tension? Are you feeling any pain? Release tension in the muscle and then keep moving.

Eventually, you'll reach the very bottom of your body. At which point you can begin to concentrate on your breathing for a while. Breathing should be 'belly breathing', which begins with the gut expanding and then fills the lungs all the way up. Breathing steadily and rhythmically will slow the heart rate via the parasympathetic nervous system and put you in an even calmer state. Finally, bring your attention to just below the navel and hold it there. This is your center of gravity and concentrating here will ground you.

Throughout this process, you might notice your thoughts start to drift from time to time. If this happens, don't let it concern you. It is normal and not the end of the world – just quietly dismiss those thoughts and then return to the focus.

Finally, repeat the steps in reverse order and bring yourself back around. That was a body scan meditation!

This is a powerful tool because it is forcing you to direct your attention and to ignore the outside thoughts. More importantly, it is engaging you with your own body, physicality and surroundings. And when you do this, your sensations become richer and more vivid.

Eventually, if you keep practicing this skill, you should get to the point where you can begin to become more mindful and more present at will – even while moving and engaging in other tasks. That means just taking a moment to actually *look* at the world around you. Pausing to see what you can hear. And fixing your posture. It means not getting so caught up in your own thoughts that you let life pass you by, or that you live in a constant state of stress and anxiety.

Once you can do this, then you will find that nothing can stir you in quiet the same way unless you want it to. You can always just enjoy being in the moment and forget the past and the future for a time. You can enjoy living and taste the amazing taste of that chocolate biscuit while that email sits there in your outbox completely unsent.

This is the key to happiness: you can *choose* to react positively instead of negatively. You can choose to view things as a challenge or an amusing hiccup instead of a serious threat. But it is also the key to unlocking your full potential so you perform better and achieve more!

Printed by Libri Plureos GmbH in Hamburg,
Germany